THE MORE SIGNIFICANT REGENCY FURNITURE 1800-1830+

A REGENCY INTERIOR IN BRISTOL SHOWING FURNITURE OF CONTEMPORARY AND EARLIER GEORGIAN DESIGNS AS EXPORTED FROM DUBLIN ESPECIALLY TO ALL NEIGHBORING COUNTIES OF ENGLAND, SCOTLAND, AND WALES.
Crown Copyright.

THE MORE SIGNIFICANT REGENCY FURNITURE
1800-1830+

BY

F. LEWIS HINCKLEY

WITH 105 ILLUSTRATIONS

A WASHINGTON MEWS BOOK
Washington Square, New York

Other books by F. Lewis Hinckley

Directory of the Historic Cabinet Woods

Directory of Queen Anne, Early Georgian & Chippendale Furniture: Establishing the Preeminence of the Dublin Craftsmen

Hepplewhite, Sheraton & Regency Furniture

Queen Anne & Georgian Looking Glasses

Metropolitan Furniture of the Georgian Years

The More Significant Georgian Furniture

© 1991 by the Estate of F. Lewis Hinckley
All rights reserved
Manufactured in the United States of America

Library of Congress Cataloging-in-Publication Data

Hinckley, F. Lewis.
   The more significant Regency furniture, 1800-1830+ / by F. Lewis Hinckley.
      p.   cm.
   ISBN 0-8147-3473-1 (cloth)
   1. Furniture, Regency—Ireland—Dublin. 2. Furniture—Ireland—Dublin—Expertising. I. Title.
NK2528.H56   1991
749.22'91835'09034—dc20   90-45238
                                                                           CIP

Contents

FOREWORD	1
REGENCY AND OTHER DUBLIN FURNITURE COLLECTED BY BRITISH ROYALTY AND SOCIETY IN GENERAL DURING THE EIGHTEENTH AND EARLY NINETEENTH CENTURY, AND AGAIN DURING THE LATER REFURBISHING OF OLD RESIDENCES	3
ILLUSTRATIONS OF DUBLIN MASTERPIECES EXHIBITED AND PUBLISHED SINCE THE TURN OF THE NINETEENTH CENTURY AS *ENGLISH*, AND LATELY AS *LONDON* PRODUCTIONS	21
INDEX	81

Foreword

OF ALL LAY WRITERS on the subject of so-called *Old English Furniture*, none has ever shown any awareness of the unadvertised trade in such masterpieces that has been carried on throughout the last hundred years. In that traffic countless numbers of choice pieces from ancestral homes in Ireland have been obtained from the Dublin antique shops, as first visited by members of British society in the refurbishing of old English residences, and then by old-time American and English dealers in antique furniture.

Nor have any of those nonprofessional authorities ever recognized the existence of Dublin in respect to its normal and indeed prolific production of high-quality furniture and looking glasses. Therefore, none has ever been able to discover the principal source of Queen Anne and Georgian masterpieces, which in all leading British and American museums are thus deprived of their true status through an inordinate number of labels mistakenly declaring them to be *ENGLISH*.

Recently those unfortunate misinterpretations have been extended by museum acceptances of obviously contrived evidences, through which a large series of typical Dublin cabinets of Regency designs have been even more imprudently published as *LONDON* productions; *vide* Plate 52. Furthermore, through the use of the names of little known or unknown London craftsmen, the most characteristic of Dublin's Hepplewhite marquetry commodes have now been published with museum sponsorship as "Made in London by Pierre Langlois"; while a large group of diverse Dublin masterpieces have all been similarly misrepresented as "Made in London by John Channon."

Therefore, in the following text attention is not entirely confined to such liberties taken in regard to those typical Dublin Regency clock-cabinets, but is also paid to those introduced in respect to the equally characteristic Dublin Hepplewhite and Chippendale productions, as these have received much greater international publicity.

Regency and Other Dublin Furniture

Collected by
British Royalty and Society in General
During the Eighteenth
and Early Nineteenth Century,
and Again During the Later
Refurbishing of Old Residences

WHILE SOME FRAGMENTARY ATTENTION has been paid to Dublin masterpieces in the academic textual treatments of so-called Old English Furniture, the major works on that supposed subject have seldom if ever been read through. Thus such information has been largely if not entirely overlooked. Indeed, it has had no perceptible effect on the authors themselves, or on any of their followers. This has been especially noticeable in respect to Dublin furniture of Regency designs, and those productions simultaneously continuing the popularity of Chippendale forms in that capital during the later Georgian years.

It is still unrecognized that during those years the more prominent Dublin makers of seat furniture, cabinetwork, and looking glasses were delivering their productions not only throughout Ireland itself, but also to some of the most important private residences in Great Britain. Nor is it realized that they were also being patronized by members of the British royal family in respect to their own imaginative creations, of which there were no satisfactory counterparts to be found in the London market.

This has been evidenced by pieces of unmistakable Dublin designs that were specially ordered from the Irish capital, such as the set of Regency brass-inlaid amboina and rosewood sofa tables recorded only as "Made in 1816 for Princess Charlotte"; *vide* my *Hepplewhite, Sheraton, and Regency Furniture*, Plate 64; and also by a similarly incontestable Sheraton inlaid satinwood breakfront bookcase recorded only as *Made for Queen Charlotte; vide* Percy Macquoid, *Age of Satinwood*, Fig. 181.

More substantial documentation was discovered in examining a pier mirror of a design usually accepted as "English, in the Adam style." This still retained the original label of one *Kearney, Carver, Gilder and Looking Glass Maker to His Majesty*—an honor rarely noted in respect to Georgian craftsmen in their entirety (*vide* my *Queen Anne and Georgian Looking Glasses*, Pl. 98). Joshua Kearney, I was able to find through the efforts of John Teahan in the National Museum of Ireland, worked in Dublin at 186 Great Britain Street from 1795 to 1805, and at 49 Henry Street to 1820.

Of still greater interest to these researches is the firm of *Mack, Williams, and Gibton*.

Their label appears on a "Chippendale" mahogany dumbwaiter "*circa* 1760," that is illustrated in the revised edition of the *Dictionary of English Furniture*. There the address is given as *39 Stafford Street*, and it is left to be assumed that the firm was located in some undeterminable English furniture center. As most Chippendale circular tripod tables and dumbwaiters have proved to be Dublin, rather than London productions, information about that partnership was again sought in that capital.

John Teahan once more assisted these researches by informing me that: "John Mack, cabinet maker, had an address at 188 Abbey Street in 1785. In the period 1794-1800 he also had an address at 39 Stafford Street. Soon after this time he began to work in partnership with another cabinet maker called Gibton and they were listed at the same addresses in 1805 and 1810. Around this time they were joined by another cabinet maker called Williams. Mack, Williams, and Gibton were listed together at 39 Stafford Street from 1815 to 1825."

The latter partnership is mentioned by Edwards and Jourdain in their listing of London craftsmen in *Georgian Cabinet-Makers* (1955), p. 102: "MACK, WILLIAMS and GIBTON. *Fl. circa 1760*. Each of a pair of fine serpentine-fronted mahogany commodes, c. 1760, with elaborate brass rococo handles, formerly in the Samuel Courtauld Collection, bears the trade label of these makers. They are described as 'Upholsterers and Cabinet Makers to His Majesty, His Excellency the Lord Lieutenant and the Rt. Hon. His Majesty's Board of Works, 39 Stratford [sic], Dublin. N. B. Auctions, Valuations and Funerals Attended.'"

Although Edwards and Jourdain could name no London craftsmen authorized to advertise themselves as *Makers to His Majesty*, they sought no further information about a firm that had been more signally honored than Thomas Chippendale, who in fact had never been patronized by the king or any other members of the royal family. Thus they and their followers continued to remain completely oblivious to the long-extended popularity of Chippendale designs in Dublin shops, and consequently throughout Ireland as a whole. Expectably, all such fine serpentine-fronted mahogany commodes, as well as their elaborate brass rococo handles, continued to be accepted as dating from circa 1760, rather than some half-century or more later, or concurrently with the regular development of Regency designs in that capital.

This same disparity applies of course to the Chippendale mahogany dumbwaiter similarly mistaken as having been produced circa 1760, and to innumerable other tables, commodes, cabinets, secretaires, and so on, all of which should be recognized as *Late Chippendale* examples. Late Georgian techtonic methods are apparent in some instances; and in some there are discrepancies in the degrees of patination and/or oxidation. Differences in overall designs and ornamental treatments may be slight. With a fine Late Chippendale carved mahogany breakfront bookcase, of the type that is routinely attributed either to William Vile or Thomas Chippendale, a suspicious professional buyer sought to obtain its history from the former owner in Scotland. He was notified that the piece had remained in the one family ever since it was first inventoried in 1825. *Vide* my *Metropolitan Furniture of the Georgian Years*, Pl. 107.

The name of Thomas Chippendale has been relentlessly associated with characteristic examples of Dublin seat furniture, cabinetwork, and looking glasses during the last hundred years. Even such recent authorities as Edwards and Jourdain have mistakenly attributed such masterpieces to his hand, merely on the basis of their "high quality." (*Vide*

Georgian Cabinet-Makers, pp. 70-71, Ills. 94-99, 101-104, 114-117, 119-121, 124, 125, 130, 133. Eventually the name of William Vile was similarly exploited: *op. cit.*, pp. 51-54, Ills. 56, 57, 64, 68, 69.) Then, in the continuing dearth of bona fide London productions, which in England are seldom relinquished from long-enduring family ownerships, additional names have been inexplicably drawn upon as supposedly suitable for associating with two separate groups of especially distinguished Dublin commodes.

Exceptionally high praise has been lavished on one group of these Dublin extravaganzas (*vide* my *Metropolitan Furniture of the Georgian Years*, Pls. 11, 12), all of which have been capriciously labeled and published as "Made in London" by one John Channon whose actual work is quite unknown. With a similar lack of responsibility each of the other group (*op. cit.*, Pl. 21), has been attributed to Pierre Langlois, whose accomplishments as a *marqueteur* were confined to an entirely different and earlier combination of inlay materials from those employed for these particular Dublin masterpieces. *Vide Georgian Cabinet-Makers*, p. 103, Pl. 227.

Some years ago the more sumptuous and most fancifully designed of the so-called *Channon* commodes was "Purchased by the [Victoria and Albert] Museum for £5,000 with the help of a substantial grant from the National Art Collections Fund and a contribution from Messrs. H. Blairmann and Sons." That appears to have been regarded as a considerable sum to have been spent, granted, and contributed toward the acquisition of a so-called London commode of such obvious superiority. However, a far greater appreciation, aesthetically and monetarily, was extended to one of the commodes in the group that, with similar irresponsibility, has been attributed to Langlois. In November of 1979 that particular masterpiece (*vide Antiques World*, February 1980, p. 32), was sold for a record price of $232,000 at auction, apparently with a view toward obtaining a substantially higher resale figure.

The height of museum nonchalance, in attempted authentifications of unrecognized Dublin masterpieces, was reached when a brass-inlaid and ormolu-mounted mahogany cabinet was attributed to John Channon, supposedly in collaboration with the heavy-handed Abraham Roentgen. To indicate the problematical nature of this particular masterpiece, the identification of which was far beyond the abilities of such unprofessional authorities, and obviously beyond that of a professional dealership, a closely related but even more exuberant example was advertised many years ago. This appeared in a catalogue issued by M. Harris, where it was described as a "Louis XIV Thuyawood Cabinet of Drawers on stand. . . . Made in France probably for the Russian Market."

Some years later a "George II mahogany Table" with identical knee and foot mounts was advertised by another English dealer, long known in the trade for his important private Irish sources of supply. It was not until the halftone illustrations and photographs of these and a few other mutually related pieces were then removed from different sections of my proving files, and finally, in 1978, grouped together for comparisons of their distinctive ormolu details, that their common origins in Dublin could be accurately established.

Museum acceptances of all the so-called Channon Pieces are based solely upon the unprecedented use of *two* metal labels that have been "discovered" on a pair of massive bookcases found in Powderham Castle, Exeter. According to an English museum keeper: "The evidence is all set out in an impressive article contributed by John Hayward to the V. & A. Museum Bulletin, Vol. 2, No. 2 (1966)."

The article, entitled "The Channon family of Exeter and London," is constructed around those two bookcases and their *two* incredible metal attachments: "Each of these is signed and dated [NB] on a brass plaque set in the middle of the door frame at the bottom. The signature[1] J. CHANNON is in Gothic lettering and is accompanied by the date 1740 [NB]." This is indeed "evidence all set out" that each and every one of the so-called Channon Pieces had been misrepresented to museum authorities, and in turn by them to the public at large, despite their clear and unequivocal Dublin designs.

The misinterpreted Channon Pieces presently consist of the following Dublin masterpieces, none of which can seriously be compared to any of the few known London productions:

(A). Two tall and heavy baroque "Germanic-looking" cabinets, *vide Country Life*, January 13, 1950; one with distinctive Dublin rococo handles that R. W. Symonds claimed were "made in Paris specially for this cabinet";
(B). The cabinet of an entirely different Dublin style and make that is described above in connection with another claimed as "Made in France";
(C). The more elegant, lavishly mounted serpentine-front commodes, also with unmistakable Dublin rococo handles. *Vide Metropolitan Furniture of the Georgian Years*, Pls. 11, 12;
(D). A solitary rosewood chair with distinctively whorled-together arm terminals and supports, a Dublin innovation,[2] (*vide A Directory of Queen Anne, Early Georgian and Chippendale Furniture*, Ills. 67, 68, 72, 87), that was never introduced in London or elsewhere.

All of those disparate examples could not possibly have been made by one man or in any one shop. This would have been especially true in respect to the unknown work of John Channon, who in leaving his provincial town is thus supposed to have immediately possessed skills akin to those acquired by the great Parisian *ébéniste*, Charles André Boulle, and also those of the equally renowned Parisian metalist, Charles Cressent.

Following the successful acceptances of the Channon Pieces another type of inscription was introduced, apparently at the direction of the same entrepreneur, to promote another large group of Dublin masterpieces, this time of closely similar Regency designs. This ruse was also easily and economically carried out, simply by having the name and address of an old London institution inscribed on the dial of an ordinary summital clock incorporated in the design of a typical Dublin clock-cabinet. The inscription: *Weekes' Museum Titchborne Street*, was accepted without question as proving that the one particular cabinet, along with at least eleven others, had all originated in London.

In those acceptances museum officials gave no thought to the fact that no museum would ever have had its name and street address marked prominently on the front of any item intended to be exhibited within its own premises; nor has it ever become customary for museum discards to be identified as such. Furthermore, the items on display in Weekes' Museum were intended to "exhibit the powers of mechanism." Had it indeed been deemed feasible for the wind-up spring movement of a clock to serve that purpose, there were innumerable larger and far more powerful clocks readily available in London. Thus it would have been absurd to acquire a large and costly secretary-cabinet to exhibit a small and wholly unremarkable summital clock that was no more than an adjunct, and of such incidental value that the dial displayed no maker's name.

The first of these cabinets to be so inscribed was illustrated in my *Directory of the Historic Cabinet Woods*, pp. 49-50 (in which the captions have been transposed). All of the details are determinative of a Dublin origin, in particular its distinctively crossetted panels of sabicu. The appearance of sabicu in any examples of Georgian cabinetwork is virtual proof of their Dublin, rather than London origins. The same use of crossetted borders framing panels of sabicu appears in Regency dwarf cabinet and in smaller Regency secretaries, such as the one illustrated (Fig. 56) in the *Dictionary of English Furniture*, where it is described as "sacquebu [sic] wood."

The amazing appearance of still another of these cabinets, imprudently flaunting the very same inscription: *Weekes' Museum Titchborne Street, vide* Ill. 94, has not caused the slightest dismay in English museum circles—even though that repetition has of course implied the ridiculously unreasonable positioning of more than one of these expensive and nearly identical tall clock-cabinets, side-by-side or otherwise, within the limited confines of that one small London museum.

The same museum furniture historian who had sent me copies of the Hayward article on the first of the so-called Channon Pieces has also devoted his attentions to the Weekes' Cabinets. About the former items he informed me that he "had seen the Powderham bookcases and regard the inscribed tablet [sic] as genuine—there are a few rare precedents [?] I think this article is well researched and answers most of your questions. About the Weekes [sic] Cabinets [he continued] I have never come across a labelled or documented example, but the silver fitments are all London marked. I have a hunch that Seddons may have been responsible for the group." My own unprejudiced hunch is that the same entrepreneur had considered silver attachments more appropriate than brass in promoting these more delicate Dublin masterpieces, which contrast sharply with the lack of individuality in Seddon's designs. *Vide Georgian Cabinet-Makers*, p. 80, Pls. 174-176.

In these first scientific comparative studies of old *British* furniture it has generally been impossible for photographic evidence to be confirmed by any other type of documentation. Thus it was a welcomed surprise to find such proof available to confirm my findings in regard to the so-called Channon Pieces. When John Hayward was persuaded to undertake his "impressive article" on John Channon, it is obvious that he did not avail himself of the meager information published some decades previously by Edwards and Jourdain. This might possibly have curbed his enthusiastic endorsement of an obvious hoax. In *Georgian Cabinet-Makers* (p. 102), these veteran observers devoted a very short article to all of the facts then known about:

"T. CHANNON
Fl. circa 1754 [NB]

'T. CHANNON, fecit', is inscribed on a [sic] brass plate attached to one [sic] of a pair of fine early Georgian mahogany bookcases with gilt enrichments at Powderham Castle, near Exeter. 'Channon senior' and 'Channon junior' appear among the subscribers to the *Director*, 1754. The address of this firm is not recorded."

Thus John Hayward would have been advised that at the time of their long-previous inspection only *one* brass plate had then been attached to just *one of a pair* of bookcases, and that the single brass plate did not show an exact date of 1740 or any date at all. Thus their

"Fl. circa 1754" was merely a guess on their part based on the date of Chippendale's *Director*. It is obvious, therefore, that the single brass plate was removed at some time between their inspection and the time when *two* brass *plaques* were found to have been attached (with new? or "antiqued" brass screws?) to the pair of bookcases, as recorded by John Hayward, both featuring the date: *1740*.

After systematically proving the Dublin designs of all the so-called Channon Pieces, and then those of the so-called Weekes' Museum Cabinets, it also became obvious that for the first time in the history of so-called *Old English Furniture* two large and important groups of unrecognized Dublin masterpieces had been brought into the London antique market through the efforts of just one particular importer; his innovative use of inscriptions on brass plates and clock dials having proved acceptable in the highest of museum circles, if not elsewhere.

From those mistaken acceptances it had also become especially clear that in spite of these and other forms of manufactured "evidence," of unfounded guesses tendered as *attributions*, or even of official documents sworn to by groups of the highest national authorities, in the consideration and evaluation of any fine antique furniture one decisive and infallible rule remains constant: *Designs Speak For Themselves*.

That rule applies most explicitly to the innumerable still unrecognized Dublin masterpieces that are currently exhibited as English in all leading British and American museums. Without those mistakenly labeled examples all such exhibitions would be reduced to displaying only the few London productions that have already been recognized, safely documented, and properly labeled.

It is also a positive fact that all Queen Anne and Georgian masterpieces of museum quality must have originated in either one or the other of the only two metropolitan furniture-producing centers in the entirety of the British Isles: either in Dublin, the most prolific, or in London. Therefore all such capital-city examples should be acknowledged according to each of their true prestigious origins, in museum labels and in all further publications on Old British Furniture; while the terms *English* and *Irish* should, henceforth, be used only in reference to provincial furniture.

Important factors in confirming the Dublin origin of Queen Anne and Georgian seat furniture and cabinetwork are the rarer cabinet woods of which some examples were made. Ormolu handles, escutcheons, and other ornamental mounts are of course of even greater significance, while sometimes even the coverings selected for seat furniture, card tables, and pole screens may help in final determinations. In respect to the cabinet woods, a considerable amount of information may be gleaned from *The Cabinet-Maker's Assistant* (London, 1853). Fortuitously this draws attention to the importance of Liverpool, far removed from London in its situation directly across the water from Dublin.

Discussing the reception there of only St. Domingo mahogany, between 1801 and 1837, p. 31: "Of the whole amount imported into Britain, nearly half is brought into Liverpool; which is resorted to not only by the chief buyers and consumers of the United Kingdom [Great Britain and Ireland, from 1801 to 1921], but is also visited by purchasers from the Continent. From the Liverpool market, France, Germany, Russia, and even India, have been drawing supplies of Spanish Mahogany."

Sabicu, *Lysiloma sabicu*, as favored in the so-called Weekes' Museum Cabinets, has generally faded from its original light brown color to paler yellowish-tan tones, much darker brown figurings sometimes resulting in its being mistaken for rosewood. Obtained in the West Indies and the Bahamas, it is not mentioned in *The Cabinet-Maker's Assistant*, and supplies may have been delivered directly to Dublin.

A different variety of sabicu is more commonly known as horseflesh mahogany. Its reddish-brown, dark red or purplish mahoganylike wood is strongly marked with darker grainy figures from which the name has been derived. To Philadelphia craftsmen such as John Gillingham it was known simply as *horse flesh:* "One pair high drawers & one dressing table, horse flesh." It is quite as rare today in extant Early American furniture as it is in that of the United Kingdom; *vide A Directory of the Historic Cabinet Woods,* Pl. 143.

A timber that has actually been recorded as having been sent from Philadelphia to Ireland is American black walnut, *Juglans nigra,* accounting for this particular, worm-free walnut in some Dublin chair frames and drawer linings. Generally of a tan or light brown color with little figure, the walnut planks obtained from southern states varied from lavender-tinted to darker purplish tones; such wood had been known as *Virginia walnut* or *black Virginia walnut* ever since the seventeenth century.

Yewwood, *Taxus baccata,* listed in the timber trade of recent decades as *Irish Yewwood,* is another of the cabinet woods that in any large-scale use is indicative of a Dublin, rather than a London production. Yew trees have survived for over two thousand years in Ireland, reaching diameters of well over three feet. The heartwood is generally distinguished by an orange-tinted, medium-brown color, though it may approach a purplish brown. The sapwood, which, like laburnum, may be utilized in combination with the heartwood, is of a creamy yellow tone. Yewwood has a fine texture, a compact cedarlike grain and takes a smooth lustrous finish.

The irregular growth of the yew, in which lower parts of the bole frequently give off new rising branches, accounts for the tiny knots that appear in the wood. At the ramifications of the branches near the roots the wood is marbled and veined in a way surpassed by few of the finest foreign woods. Occasionally burls add to these more highly figured sections of timber, developing in irregular hemispherical formations that may extend for seven feet or more along the trunk. Imperfections in wood of either type are filled with patches of sounder nature, which are often seen in examples of old Dublin cabinetwork.

After proving the designs of earlier Irish yewwood Windsor armchairs, confirmation of those displayed in the many remaining, later, high-back tavern chairs (Ill. 98) as resulting from those particular Dublin style developments was found in *The Cabinet-Maker's Assistant,* p. 39: "The importance attached to this wood, and the chief inducement to its cultivation in former times—the manufacture of bows—have now ceased for centuries. It has unfortunately fallen into undeserved neglect, and has not been extensively planted with a view to its use in the arts. At present it is not to be procured in sufficient quantity, to be made generally available for the larger articles of furniture."

Laburnum, *Cytisus laburnum,* Linn, is a wood not used in London furniture and not mentioned in *The Cabinet-Maker's Assistant.* It received some favor in Dublin furniture of Early Georgian and Chippendale designs, while some later examples, in not meeting metropolitan standards, were apparently produced outside of the capital city. As a small tree growing to heights of about twenty feet, the heartwood varies from golden-brown tones, sometimes tinged with green or red; the sapwood being of a whitish- or yellowish-tan color. The striped effects achieved with laburnum veneers are similar to those of plumwood in Parisian *ébénisterie,* and of yewwood cut to display the same contrasts.

Dublin designs are unmistakable in laburnum card tables with round tapered legs of laburnum heartwood, yew, or walnut, headed by slightly raised lappets, and finishing in pad feet; *vide* R. W. Symonds, *Furniture-Making in 17th and 18th Century England,* Fig. 170. It was also used for occasional tables, pembroke tables, dressing tables, dressing mirrors, and chests of drawers, some of which retain the original, confirming handles and escutcheons. Similarly identifying mounts, in silver, distinguish a particularly elegant Chippendale coffret-on-stand illustrated (Fig. 90) in *A Directory of the Historic Cabinet Woods.* Favorite Dublin lattice-work patterns also characterize laburnumwood armchairs and open shelves of Chinese-Chippendale designs.

Bird's-eye maple is another of the American timbers received in Dublin. The *Cabinet-Maker's Assistant* praised it as "one of the most beautiful materials employed in the manufacture of cabinet furniture." As "the wood of *Acer saccharinum,* the sugar maple, rock maple, or hard maple; it is indigenous to America, and is found in greatest abundance...in the northern parts of the States of New York and Pennsylvania, and in Canada.... The figure in maple of the highest repute is that known under the name of 'bird's-eye'—a designation which it has acquired from the small dots, or little conical projections, with a small hollow in the centre, which, in the finished work, bear a strong resemblance to the eye of a bird."

In Dublin these veneers were employed in the surfacing of Sheraton and Regency tables and desks of various forms, with bandings or narrow borders of ebony or other dark or dark-stained woods. Similar contrasting effects were also carried out to set off areas of bird's-eye maple in American furniture of the Early Federal years. With a somewhat later appreciation in England, maple and bird's-eye maple were used in the manufacture of mirror and picture frames, and for "the interior fittings of Davenport writing desks, or similar articles of drawing-room furniture, which require to be nicely finished internally."

Padauk is another rare cabinet wood that, like sabicu, is not treated in *The Cabinet-Maker's Assistant.* This may have been because its former use in England a century earlier than 1853 was either unknown or no longer considered worthy of mention. It was in fact used by William Masters of London, who between 1749 and 1756 supplied his furniture for the Duke of Athol at Blair Castle; and it appears in Queen Charlotte's jewel cabinet, made by William Vile in 1761, *vide Georgian Cabinet-Makers* (1955) Pl. 62. Among their still undiscovered Dublin compeers, padauk was more popular and received a more extended favor, appearing here in the Regency dining table, Pl. 8.

Andaman padauk, *Ptercarpus dalbergiodes,* is generally of a rich, deep reddish-brown or crimson color with darker red or black streaks. Burmese padauk, *P. macrocarpus,* is quite similar, but fades with age to a more golden-brown color than the Andaman timber. The two varieties cannot always be distinguished except through microscopic examination of their cell patterns. The name has frequently been misspelled as "padouk." Thus it is also mispronounced as "pa*duke,*" rather than as "pa dauk" or pa *dowk.*"

Rosewood was obtained from various trees of the genus *Jacaranda,* the name by which the wood is known in northern Europe. Principal supplies were shipped from Brazil. The color varies from reddish-brown to purplish-brown tones, and the wood is streaked and variegated with black. In Late Georgian and especially Regency furniture it often displays a more subdued brownish effect, as in the card table in Illustration 42. From the earlier designs of certain pieces received in the London antique market, it would appear that Dublin extended some favor to rosewood long before it became popular in London.

The Early Georgian rosewood commode with lion's-paw feet that had been illustrated (Fig. 128) in Macquoid's *Age of Mahogany* passed through my hands some thirty years ago. At the time I was interested in its open-mouthed satyr-head escutcheons reflecting Scandinavian influence. I could not have anticipated at that time the future importance of its far more characteristic Dublin-rococo ormolu handles. These would eventually be considered by R. W. Symonds, as they appeared on pieces not yet promoted as "by John Channon," as impossible for him to accept as *English*.

The Early Georgian armchair included in those later Channon acceptances as supposedly made in 1740 or thereabouts is also illustrative of an early Dublin use of rosewood, especially so as its particular whorled-together arm terminals and supports preceded the modified treatments later employed in respect to Dublin Chippendale seat furniture.

Holly, *Ilex aquifolium*, Linn, as a shrub or tree is widely distributed on the Continent, in the British Isles, and in North America. It appears occasionally as sizable veneer panels in fine Dublin, London, and Baltimore cabinetwork. The tree grows to about fifty feet in height and from two to four feet in diameter. The wood is of a chalky-white or ivory tone, very hard, uniform and close in grain, and takes a fine polish. It is apt to split when first cut and in seasoning; it is also difficult to prepare for use as veneers, which, as backgrounds for marquetry work, have often developed hairline cracks. These veneers have frequently been accepted as satinwood despite the fact that they display no satinlike effects.

Similar mistakes have been made in regard to holly and even boxwood by lay writers in describing such inlays as "satinwood bandings" or "satinwood stringing lines." The narrower inlays are referred to in *The Cabinet-Maker's Assistant* under *Holly*: "It admits of being dyed of various colors with great facility. It was formerly much used, chiefly in the white stage, or when dyed black, for lines of 'stringing' in cabinet work." Boxwood, *Buxus sempervirens*, Linn, is also very close grained and hard, but tougher, heavier, and of a yellower tone than holly. After its use in borders of Late Stuart cabinetwork it was largely replaced by holly, apparently accounting for the fact that it is not mentioned in *The Cabinet-Maker's Assistant*.

With the increasing popularity of knob and loose-ring handles in Regency cabinetwork, often accompanied by simple brass keyhole surrounds rather than ornamental escutcheons, these particular accessories are usually of no real value in the confirming of Dublin designs. Thus, whereas the distinguishing ornamental fittings of the so-called Channon and Langlois pieces provided positive proof of their Dublin designs, the insignificant handles and escutcheons of the so-called Weekes' Museum Cabinet (Pl. 52) were of no value whatsoever toward identifying or confirming its true origin.

The most distinctive of these fittings among the present illustrations are those of the chest-of-drawers (Pl. 45) and the drum table (Pl. 30). The oval patera handles of the former piece are representative of the continuing excellence of Dublin ormolu work, invariably described as "reflecting the finest skills of the English metal worker." The more fanciful escutcheons are of a rare pattern that appeared on a bombé dressing cabinet removed from an old Irish residence. In spite of R. W. Symonds's assertion that "if a piece is known to have come out of Ireland it is accepted as having been made there"[3] a photograph of that piece remained in an "unproven" file until the chest-of-drawers, with its own determinative set of escutcheons, finally supplied the long-awaited confirmative evidence.

The stellular knob handles, anthemion escutcheons, pearl-chain moldings, and top edging of the drum table (Ill. 64) have provided such evidence in the proving of this and many other Regency tables, especially sofa tables, one of which is illustrated (Fig. 187) in R. W. Symonds, *Furniture Making in 17th and 18th Century England*. These tables have in turn featured other Dublin forms, as well as additional ormolu fittings such as the *sabots*, or toe caps, and leafy knee mounts of the center table (Ill. 29). Ormolu panel-moldings composed of C-scrolls, as in Plate 17, are repeated in a rosewood dressing table with Egyptian terms owned by the Duke of Wellington (Fig. 222 in Margaret Jourdain, *Regency Furniture*). The very same ormolu patterns that were used on sofa tables may also appear on Dublin cabinets, the frieze mounts of Illustration 37 being repeated on the pilasters of an important rosewood bookcase illustrated (Fig. 86) in Jourdain and Rose, *English Furniture: The Georgian Period*.

Of all the ornamental techniques that should be considered in determining the provenance of Regency furniture, the patterns of Dublin[4] and London ormolu work have still not received the attentions of museum authorities or equally unprofessional lay writers on the subject of *Old English Furniture*. None has been able to recognize even the most characteristic of Dublin rococo handles, such as those claimed by R. W. Symonds as "made in Paris." Thus, where a piece such as the ebony cabinet (Pl. 53) is almost entirely dependent on its ormolu accessories for ornamental relief, a similar lack of perception might just as willfully result in its misinterpretation as a Parisian example of *circa* 1825-1835. A final determination in these studies was withheld until a rosewood dressing table of an unmistakable Dublin design appeared, featuring an exactly matching pair of ormolu nymphs with cymbals. From such insistent leanings toward supposedly Parisian patterns in bronze doré a number of Dublin productions (as Ill. 45) have also been attributed to the hand of the French *ébéniste* Charles Honoré Lannuier, during his short stay in New York City.

The chairs (Ills. 13-15) loaned to a 1905 exhibition of Old English Furniture by Sir Spencer Ponsonby Fane, and indeed all of the heirlooms that he and his wife brought over from Ireland when they settled in Brympton D'Enercy, Somerset, were a source of encouragement during the early years of these researches. When an uninterrupted series of Sir Spencer's pieces, as illustrated by contemporary authorities, all proved to be *Irish* instead of *English*, rather than risk any possibility of errors I turned to his genealogical records. I then found that I had indeed been quite correct in judging Sir Spencer's lineage, as well as his supposedly *English* furniture.

The Fane heirlooms continued to receive wide publicity throughout the first half of the present century, those represented in my proving files being too numerous to mention here. Suffice to say that starting with the so-called *Charles II* and *William III* lacquer cabinets on baroque stands, as illustrated by Percy Macquoid, *Age of Walnut*, (Figs. 127 and 131) and extending through Queen Anne, Early Georgian, Chippendale, and Late Georgian masterpieces, all are just as thoroughly representative of the designs created in Dublin as they are atypical of those produced in London.

Among the Fane heirlooms at Brympton D'Enercy was a set of six Early Georgian walnut upholstered side chairs, each with all four cabriole legs headed by scrolls projecting above the upholstered seatframe, and finishing in doubly molded, whorled feet. Also in

The More Significant Regency Furniture

typical Dublin fashion, the front legs are boldly carved with leaf scrolls, frilled rosettes, and foliage pendants. Apparently part of a former family assemblage, these chairs are representative of an unusually large Dublin production of stools, side chairs, and armchairs, some suites carried out in walnut, and others in mahogany. None of these pieces was ever labeled, but Sir Spencer's chairs were all stamped with the maker's initials: W. F.

One armchair of this abundant production was published by Percy Macquoid, *Age of Mahogany* (Fig. 104) as bearing a label through which it was also accepted by R. W. Symonds, Edwards and Jourdain, and, as having been designed and produced in London by Giles Grendy. According to Edwards and Jourdain (*Georgian Cabinet-Makers*, pp. 47-48): "A number of chairs and stools exist, having legs similar to the upholstered chair bearing Grendy's label, and, as this design is unusual it may be inferred [sic] that those specimens came from his shop."

However, in this case also, it happens that once again Dublin designs speak for themselves. No other Grendy advertisement or label has ever appeared on any other single piece of seat furniture even remotely resembling the design of the legs in that Dublin production, or that of the arms and their supports, which are distinctively carved with ribbed leafage rising to rosetted arm terminals, also in characteristic Dublin fashion.

Although it in no way resembles either the design or type of carving that distinguished that particular Dublin armchair, some museum experts have used it as a basis for attributing an entire group of heirloom furniture to the same London craftsman. This is the well-known suite of upholstered side chairs, settees with typical Dublin eagle-head arm terminals, and card tables, all with characteristic Irish petit-point needlework coverings. The legs of the entire suite are headed by lion masks with flanking rosetted leaf scrolls and frills, and finished in paw feet. The suite has been illustrated in color in the *Dictionary of English Furniture* and elsewhere as the property of Lord DeLisle and Dudley, Copped Hall, Essex, or Penshurst Place, Kent—who was also the inheritor of various other Dublin masterpieces.

Heirloom pieces, unrecognized as having originated in Dublin, together with the naiveté of lay authorities in their bafflement over such unstudied designs, always bring to mind their resulting inferences, surmises, attributions, and other wrong guesses, through which they have managed to obliterate the very name of London's sister capital from the literature. Thus, in also failing to recognize the furniture ordered from Dublin by the fourth Duke of Beaufort for Badminton House in Gloucestershire, Edwards and Jourdain (*Georgian Cabinet-Makers*, p. 71) claim that "All these pieces are of conspicuously high quality, and while there is no definite evidence, the Duke's subscription to the *Director* and date of the group would seem to point to Chippendale's responsibility." [!]

In also being unaware of a general recourse to Dublin rather than London during the latter decades of the nineteenth century[5] for the refurbishing of old English residences, the same authorities (p. 70) describe the Dublin purchases then made by Lord St. Oswald to augment the furniture supplied by Thomas Chippendale to the original owner of Nostel Priory: "The late Lord St Oswald acquired some eighteenth-century seat furniture about 1883. Among these is a set consisting of a ribband back settee and six chairs which are based on the first of three designs for ribband backs given in the *Director* (first edition), and, being of high quality, may reasonably [sic!] be assigned to Chippendale." The reasonableness or sound judgment of these authorities has of course never been questioned by their similarly uninformed peers. For any of the more knowledgeable of the currently active *professionals* to do so, singly or as a group, could only prove harmful to their continuing relationships with museum officials, especially those who have been induced to promote the Channon, Langlois, and Weekes' Museum pieces so incorrectly as *London* productions.

Dependence on Dublin, rather than London, for the furnishings of fine and important homes and castles in western areas of Great Britain is also indicated in the Frontispiece. The port of Bristol, in southwest Gloucestershire on the Avon river near the Severn estuary, was of course convenient to Badminton House in that same county. Its prosperity was dependent on its ships and trade by sea, with docks spreading out from the mouth of the Avon and reaching into the heart of the town. The photograph was taken in one of its fine Georgian houses, bought by the city and furnished in its original style to show how the wealthy Bristol merchant once lived. The Early Georgian side chairs, the two Chippendale side chairs, and the Chippendale armchair are all unmistakably Dublin productions, as are apparently the sideboard and other pieces. Exceptionally fine Dublin commodes mounted in ormolu have been published as formerly contained in Blaise Castle, Bristol and in Newton Park, Bristol.

The rarest and most splendid of Dublin's fanciful creations, such as the Victoria and Albert Museum's elaborately mounted commode mistakenly claimed as "made in London by John Channon," must have been too highly regarded as heirlooms, or too greatly admired for their ornamental values, to have been obtainable from owners of old Irish residences during the early decades of the present century. Thus, while Percy Macquoid was working on his monumental series of volumes on *English* furniture, he was unaware of such imaginatively designed productions. Then too, when he illustrated and described any of the imported heirlooms, the names of their original or later owners meant no more to him than their unrecognized capital-city designs.

In his *Age of Mahogany* he illustrated (Fig. 9) a Georgian eagle console as made *circa* 1700, as representing "the best of English carving of the time," and as then owned by Lady North and R. Eden Dickson. Two such "superbly carved and gilded eagle side tables, (c. 1730-50)," but with flanking satyr-head monopodia, have been published as owned by the Earl of Shaftesbury, St. Giles House, Dorset; and in a magazine article ("Eagle Pier-Tables"), R. W. Symonds showed "A pair of eagle tables of the finest quality, the work of a London craftsman of the first rank." The first two owners, and the descendants of the Earl of Shaftesbury, were inheritors of various Dublin productions that have been illustrated in the literature on *Old English Furniture*.

"Georgian" is the safest term applicable to such Dublin eagle consoles in general, for while they may date from the middle decades of the eighteenth century, this is by no means invariable. A later version has been published as "One of a pair of magnificent Chippendale giltwood eagle Console Tables of outstanding importance, superbly carved throughout; surmounted by Siena marble tops...Formerly at Duchray Castle, Aberfoyle, Perthshire." Also of a late date, coinciding with the production of Late Chippendale and Regency designs, is the example here (Pl. 36), with metal bracing rods helping to support the marble slab.

An important part of these particular researches has been the indentification of heirloom pieces with their original owners if possible, and with the names of family members to whom they have descended. Titles alone can also point to the origin of such

The More Significant Regency Furniture

pieces, as that of the Dowager Countess of Limerick. Her Black Lacquer Cabinet decorated with bouquets of flowers in natural colors (Fig. 22 in the *Dictionary of English Furniture*) has obviously received no special attention from museum furniture historians. That distinguished production has been instrumental in proving the Dublin side tables of Early Georgian designs, as well as a whole series of other cabinets and secretaires decorated with the same type of floral arrangements, rather than the more usual landscapes with figures and animals of incorrectly designated Charles II and William III examples.

The geographical situations of family seats have also been serviceable. More detailed attention to the listing of original collections, inheritors, and present-day collectors of Dublin masterpieces is given in my project on *Hepplewhite, Sheraton, and Regency Furniture*.

The most revered collector of Dublin masterpieces during the present century, Queen Mary, acquired a Regency tea table similar to the one shown here in Plate 26. Her excellent and truly eclectic taste is reflected in the selection of that choice piece, which she obtained as a refurbishment for Buckingham Palace. Through the courtesy of Trevor, London, a third example is shown in the above project (Ill. 352). Actually resembling the *Directoire gueridons* that were popularized in Paris and then copied with varying treatments in Holland and elsewhere in Europe, Continental influence to any great degree, while often noticeable in such Dublin rarities, is seldom so striking in London productions.

During the turn of the eighteenth century Dublin cabinetmakers were fitting certain pieces of Sheraton and Regency designs with machine-made lever locks. These were not made locally but were obtained from London, where they were first made by Joseph Bramah, and then by Chubb, Hobbs, and others. Their use in pieces such as the wine cooler (Ill. 54) aids in refuting the absurd mid-eighteenth century date given to another such Regency example illustrated (Fig. 163) in Jourdain and Rose, *English Furniture: The Georgian Period*. The small circular escutcheon used with lever locks also appears in the Regency tambour desk (Pl. 33), and in the Sheraton satinwood secretaire that Macquoid illustrated in color with its original convex mirrors, which have been replaced with clear glass plates (Pl. 38). Since the earliest 1900s various examples of cabinetwork have been exhibited and published as dating from the original Chippendale period, *circa* 1750, despite the appearance of such keyhole plates and original lever locks, confirming their *Late Chippendale* designs of *circa* 1800-1830.

Lever locks were apparently ordered only as needed by individual cabinetmakers in Dublin, and it seems possible that they were not stocked for resale in that capital. Certainly they were plentifully available in London to any possible American purchasers. The fact that they do not appear in Early Federal cabinetwork may be just one more indication that American furniture makers had little commerce with London.

The closest relationships were those maintained among makers of seat furniture, with working patterns brought over to this country by Dublin-trained joiners for chair frames, splats, shoe pieces, and arm supports. American cabinetwork does not reflect such a close affinity with Dublin productions, and the two examples sold as American (Ills. 85 and 97) should not have been acceptable to former collectors, who allowed themselves to be misled by old-time—importing—dealers in Americana.

Designs of eighteenth- and early-nineteenth century Dublin Windsor chairs may be traced through the various stages of their development, all culminating in that of the tavern chair (Ill. 98). Such a lavish expenditure of yew would not have been feasible in England during the middle of the nineteenth century.

The Chippendale side chair (Ill. 99) is one of a large nineteenth-century set that was auctioned in three lots of eight. One set was bought by an antique dealer of the highest repute among his wealthy clients and also with his New York City peers. He immediately delivered the set to a trusting, nationally known collector as containing all genuine eighteenth-century examples. Thus that particular set of eight was necessarily billed at a commensurate figure representing an enormous profit. Two armchairs that had been included in the large original set were held over for a later sale, since they were marred by unattractive typically mid-Victorian shell-form arm terminals.

The following illustration (Pl. 57) is of a piece supplied with affidavits attesting to the fact that Dublin was not the only capital city to have its furniture claimed as English. The owner may have confused its manufacture in the later *1800*s with an impossible date in the later *18*th century. No matter what it was that moved him to do so, he had the piece packed up and shipped over to France to find out from native authorities just when and where it had actually been made. In Paris it was indeed vetted, and for his trouble, two-way shipping expenses, and the fees charged for their special expertise by *le bon* Albert, Marcel et Bernard, he was rewarded with the following reports:

> I, the undersigned, Albert Goumain, master joiner-ébéniste, expert of the tribunal, former member of the tribunal of commerce of Seine, commandant of the Legion of Honor.... Because of the composition and the style made by dissimilar elements, the appearance of this furniture is of English style....
>
> I, the undersigned, Marcel Heim, expert of the Court of Appeal and of the Tribunal Civil of Seine, declare that.... The thing in question...is of English make....
>
> I, the undersigned, Bernard Dilee, expert at the Court of Appeal and Tribunal Civil of Seine.... The thing in question is therefore a work executed towards the end of the 19 century by a foreign ébéniste very likely an Englishman, who has mixed the different elements of the style of Louis XVI.

On its return to this country, in a dockside examination I found the piece to have been made in France around 1875. I was given no impression of whether or not a lawyer on the site could fully comprehend my reasons for arriving at the same convictions as that under which the piece had been sold. However, it soon proved unnecessary to give this any further consideration. A few days later I suddenly recalled seeing an engraved illustration of the very piece. Turning in my own library to a thin pamphlet entitled *Les Artes des Bois*, published in Paris in 1891, I found a picture of the very same model, exact in every detail, over a caption reading: "Bonheur du Jour; Style Louis XVI, Garniture de Bronze Cisele et Doré, Par. M. Beurdeley." Under that name the firm had been established in Paris prior to 1875, after which it was headed by M. Beurdeley's son, Alfred.

As an addendum to the information on Late Chippendale seat furniture and cabinetwork produced during the Sheraton, Regency and Later Georgian years, the Chippendale features of the wall mirror (Pl. 58) contrast decidedly with the figural and more delicate foliated ornamental details that were not introduced in Dublin until the early nineteenth century, when they might be featured on Regency tables of various types.

The mirror reappeared in the New York antique market when The Benjamin Sonnenberg Collection was sold by Sotheby Parke-Bernet in June of 1979, and was catalogued as "North German or Danish, *circa* 1765." That description also disagrees with a cardinal rule in the judging of antique furniture, which is that *no piece can be older than its latest feature of design, construction or ornamentation*, to which may be added: *or that of any originally supplied accessories.*

Despite their un-English designs, chairs such as the two in yewwood (Ills. 102-103), and the pair of armchairs (Ills. 104-105), in which the wood had been described as *padauk*, have ever since 1905 been mistakenly accepted as Westmorland or Yorkshire productions. The yewwood chairs were found in Ireland. Thus, according to the regularly confirmed advice of R. W. Symonds, the most widely respected authority on Old English Furniture, that: "If a piece is known to have come out of Ireland it is accepted as having been made there"; in addition to the Dublin patterns of the arms, arm terminals, and supports, and the favorite but in this instance rare use of yewwood in the particular making, they were apparently produced in that capital city.

Surprisingly, wood pegs appear in the underframing of the yew side chair (Ill. 103), as they do also in the pair of armchairs described as made of padauk, and where the shallow seat frames were never intended for upholstering in the European fashion. In these armchairs the lowest framing members are also atypical of Georgian seat furniture in general, while in their unseen portions they are marked with Chinese characters. If the wood was indeed padauk, more favored in Dublin than in London furniture, that would indicate the unlikely presence of Chinese craftsmen in Europe during the Regency years, for padauk, native to the Andaman Islands and Burma, is not indigenous to China. However, the wood is probably East Indian rosewood, quite similar to padauk in surface coloring and graining, if not in feel when cut. This would establish their production in Canton or elsewhere in southern China, where large supplies of that particular timber were received from India and Ceylon, even before it was introduced in Europe during the early nineteenth century.

---

1. To an unbiased researchist or professionally trained appraiser a *signature* can be interpreted only as *The name of a person written in his own hand.*
2. As an *Irish* innovation, recognized as far back as 1906 by Percy Macquoid, Age of Mahogany, Figs. 100, 101.
3. While this was a tardy acknowledgment of such high-quality furniture being exported from Ireland, Symonds was never able to recognize a single Dublin design among the many such masterpieces that he illustrated as from the famous Percival Griffiths collection, or those brought to his attention by the few London importers whom he patronized.
4. From the Dublin, rather than London patterns of handles used on furniture produced by the Gillow factory in Lancaster (pop: 9,030 by 1815) it is obvious that they were made in the advantageously situated capital city. *Vide Georgian Cabinet-Makers* (1955), Figs. 188, 191, 194.
5. At the time that Lady Churchill during her Ireland years (1877-1881) was able to obtain choice pieces from ancestral homes in her rounds of the Dublin antique shops. *Vide* Ralph G. Martin, *Jennie*, 1969.

Illustrations of Dublin Masterpieces

Exhibited and Published since
the Turn of the Nineteenth Century
as *English*, and Lately even
as *London* Productions

PLATE 1

1   REGENCY INLAID AND DECORATED ARMCHAIR.

2   REGENCY PAINTED, DECORATED, AND PARCEL-GILDED ARMCHAIR.

3   REGENCY ARMCHAIR WITH PAINTED DECORATION. Collection of J. Pierpont Morgan, 1877-1913.

4   REGENCY CARVED, PAINTED, AND DECORATED ARMCHAIR. Victoria & Albert Museum. Crown Copyright.

PLATE 2

5   REGENCY CARVED MAHOGANY SIDE CHAIR.

6   REGENCY SIDE CHAIR WITH MARQUETRY DECORATION.

7   REGENCY INLAID AND DECORATED SATINWOOD ARMCHAIR. Courtesy of Trevor, London.

8   REGENCY MAHOGANY ARMCHAIR.

PLATE 3

9 REGENCY MAHOGANY ARMCHAIR ATTRIBUTED TO A PHILADELPHIA ORIGIN.

10 REGENCY INLAID MAHOGANY SIDE CHAIR.

11 REGENCY MAHOGANY ARMCHAIR.

12 REGENCY MAHOGANY ARMCHAIR.

PLATE 4

13 REGENCY PAINTED SIDE CHAIR WITH ORMOLU MOUNTS. Collection of Sir Spencer Ponsonby Fane, K.C.B.

14 REGENCY MAHOGANY ARMCHAIR WITH ORMOLU MOUNTS. Collection of Sir Spencer Ponsonby Fane, K.C.B.

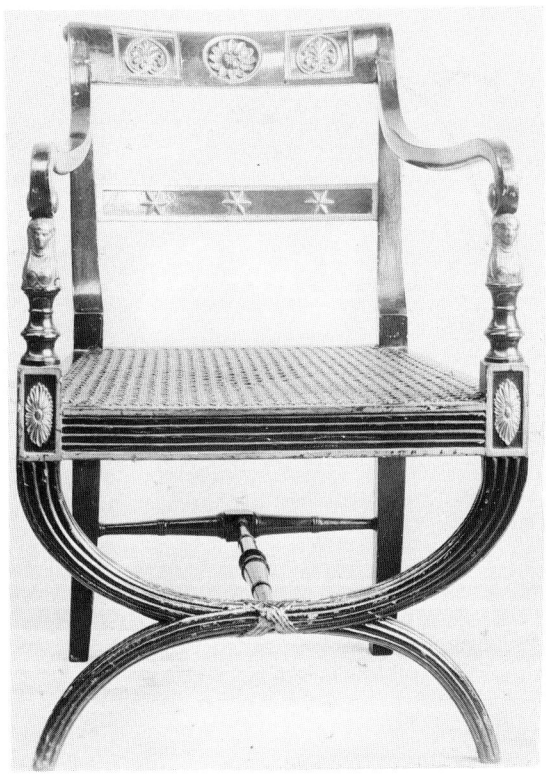

15 REGENCY PAINTED AND PARCEL-GILDED CURULE ARMCHAIR. Collection of Sir Spencer Ponsonby Fane, K.C.B.

PLATE 5

16 REGENCY BLACK-AND-GOLD SIDE CHAIR WITH EGYPTIAN-STYLE DECORATION.

17 REGENCY DECORATED BLACK-AND-GOLD SIDE CHAIR.

18 REGENCY DECORATED BLACK-AND-GOLD SIDE CHAIR.

19 REGENCY DECORATED BLACK-AND-GOLD ARMCHAIR.

PLATE 6

20 REGENCY PAINTED AND DECORATED ARMCHAIR.

21 REGENCY DECORATED BLACK-AND-GOLD ARMCHAIR.

22 REGENCY DECORATED BLACK-AND-GOLD SIDE CHAIR.

23 REGENCY BLACK-AND-GOLD ARMCHAIR WITH ORMOLU MOUNTS.

PLATE 7

24 REGENCY MAHOGANY TUB CHAIR.

25 REGENCY CARVED AND GILDED
UPHOLSTERED ARMCHAIR. Cf.
Margaret Jourdain, *Regency Furniture*,
Fig. 58.

PLATE 8

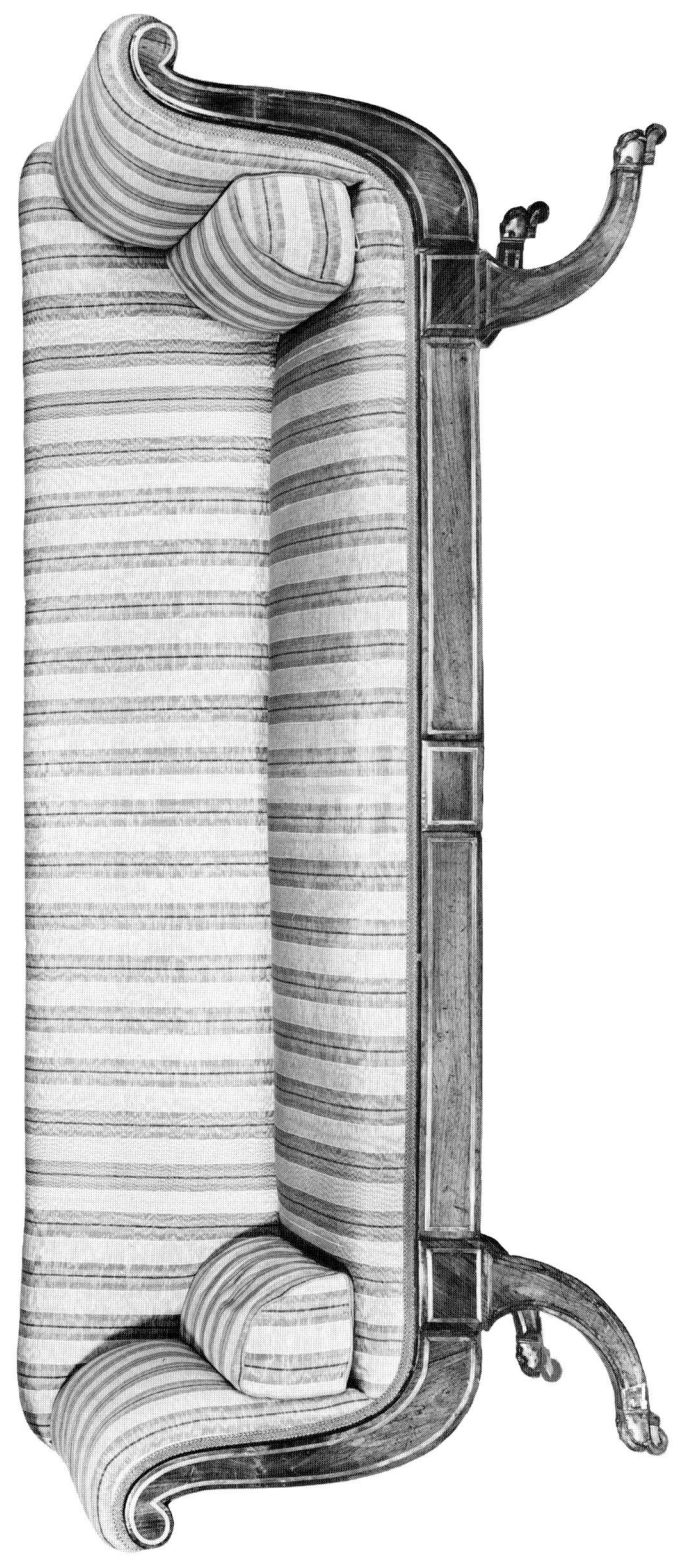

26 REGENCY BRASS-INLAID PADAUK SETTEE. Courtesy of Needham's Antiques, Inc., New York City.

PLATE 9

27 GEORGE III MAHOGANY KIDNEY-SHAPED TRIPOD READING STAND. Courtesy of J. J. Wolff (Antiques) Ltd., London and New York.

28 REGENCY MAHOGANY TILT-TOP PILLAR TABLE.

PLATE 10

29 REGENCY INLAID ROSEWOOD PILLAR TABLE. With distinctive ormolu frieze molding, knee mounts and toe caps.

30 REGENCY INLAID CALAMANDER CENTER TABLE WITH ORMOLU MOUNTS.

PLATE 11

31 REGENCY ROSEWOOD LIBRARY TABLE MOUNTED IN ORMOLU. Cf. *Dictionary of English Furniture*, Fig. 38.

32 REGENCY MAHOGANY DRUM TABLE.

PLATE 12

33 REGENCY MAHOGANY REVOLVING TRIPOD BOOKSTAND. Cf. Margaret Jourdain, *Regency Furniture*, Fig. 158.

PLATE 13

34 REGENCY MAHOGANY TWO-PEDESTAL DINING TABLE.

PLATE 14

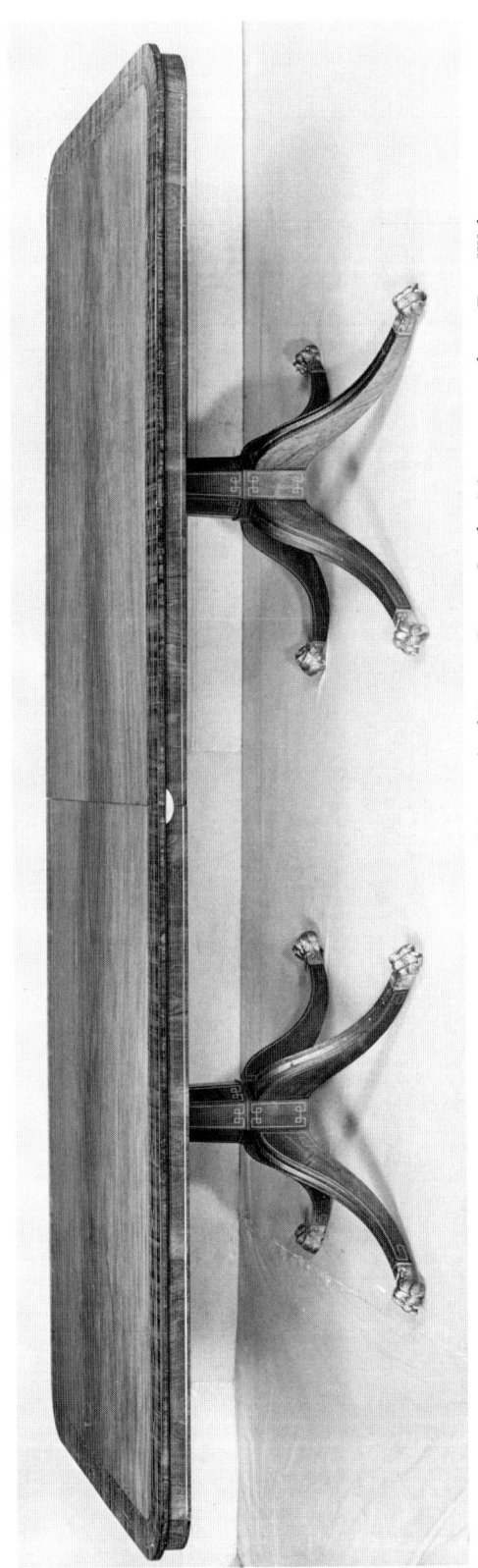

35 REGENCY INLAID SABICU TWO-PEDESTAL DINING TABLE. Collection of the Earl of Powis, Powis Castle, Montgomeryshire, East Wales.

PLATE 15

36 REGENCY INLAID MAHOGANY SOFA TABLE.

37 REGENCY INLAID ROSEWOOD SOFA TABLE MOUNTED IN ORMOLU. *Vide* identical mounts on bookcase, Jourdain & Rose, *English Furniture: The Georgian Period*, 86, "Probably by Thomas Hope."

PLATE 16

38   REGENCY INLAID ROSEWOOD AND HOLLY SOFA TABLE.

PLATE 17

39 NELSONIAN INLAID ROSEWOOD DOLPHIN SOFA TABLE. The ormolu panel moldings as those on the Duke of Wellington's dressing table with Egyptian terms; *vide* Margaret Jourdain, *Regency Furniture*, Fig. 222. Courtesy of Admiralty House, Whitehall. Photograph: Brighton Borough Council.

PLATE 18

40 REGENCY INLAID ROSEWOOD CARD TABLE. Courtesy of Needham's Antiques, Inc., New York City.

41 REGENCY BRASS-INLAID ROSEWOOD CARD TABLE. With hemispherical support that has been claimed as a Salem innovation.

PLATE 19

42 REGENCY INLAID ROSEWOOD CARD TABLE WITH ORMOLU MOUNTS.

43 REGENCY CARVED AND GILDED EAGLE CONSOLE. Courtesy of French & Co., Inc., New York City.

PLATE 20

44 REGENCY PARCEL-GILDED MAHOGANY CHINOISERIE TABLE WITH DOLPHIN SUPPORTS. Courtesy of Mallet & Son (Antiques) Ltd., London and Geneva.

PLATE 21

45 REGENCY PARCEL-GILDED ROSEWOOD MIRROR-BACK PIER TABLE WITH ORMOLU MOUNTS; ATTRIBUTED TO HONORÉ LANNUIER, NEW YORK CITY. Cf. Margaret Jourdain, *Regency Furniture*, Fig. 106, an equally typical mirror-back example "From the Earl of Caledon, Caledon, Ireland." Courtesy of The Brooklyn Museum. Gift of the Pierpont Family.

41

PLATE 22

46 LATE GEORGIAN MAHOGANY CUTLERY AND PLATE STAND.

47 LATE GEORGIAN BRASS-BOUND MAHOGANY PLATE STAND.

48 LATE GEORGIAN BRASS-BOUND MAHOGANY WINE BUCKET.

49 LATE GEORGIAN MAHOGANY WINE COOLER.

PLATE 23

50 REGENCY INLAID MAHOGANY CELLARETTE.

51 REGENCY INLAID AND PARCEL-GILDED MAHOGANY CELLARETTE OWNED BY LORD NELSON. Closed view: *Dictionary of English Furniture.* Vol. 1, 222. Courtesy of the National Maritime Museum, London.

PLATE 24

53 REGENCY MAHOGANY CELLARETTE.

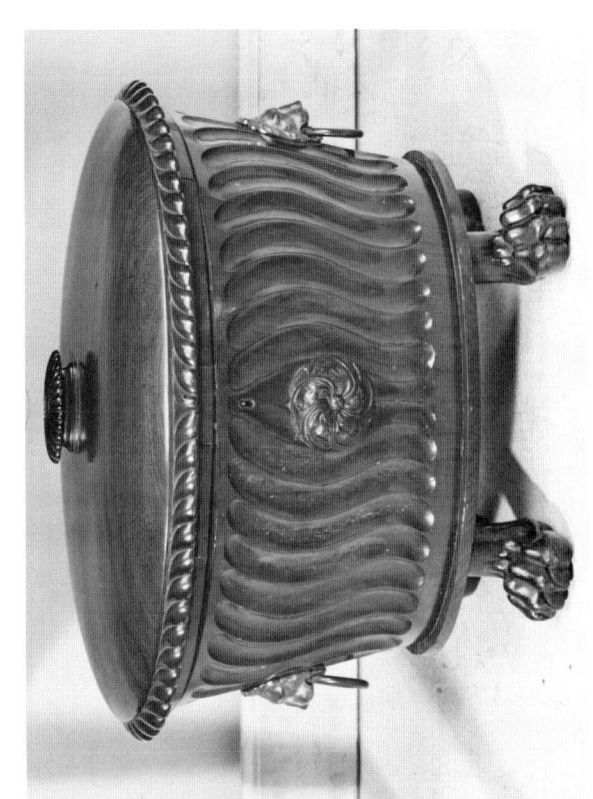

55 REGENCY MAHOGANY CELLARETTE.

52 REGENCY MAHOGANY CELLARETTE.

54 REGENCY MAHOGANY CELLARETTE. With original lever lock; a similar example, Jourdain & Rose, *English Furniture: The Georgian Period*, 163, dated as "Mid-eighteenth century." Vide also *Country Life*, Nov. 30th, 1935, 86, "Regency Furniture at Castlecoole."

PLATE 25

57 REGENCY INLAID AND DECORATED OCTAGONAL WORK TABLE.

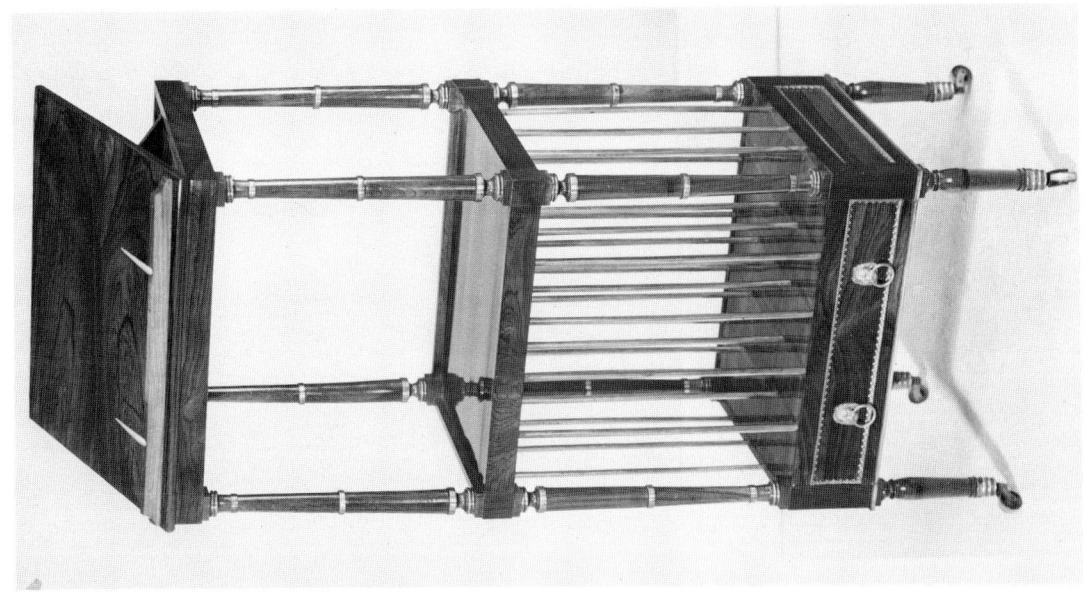

58 REGENCY ROSEWOOD AND ORMOLU OPEN-SHELF STAND WITH READING LEDGE AND CANTERBURY.

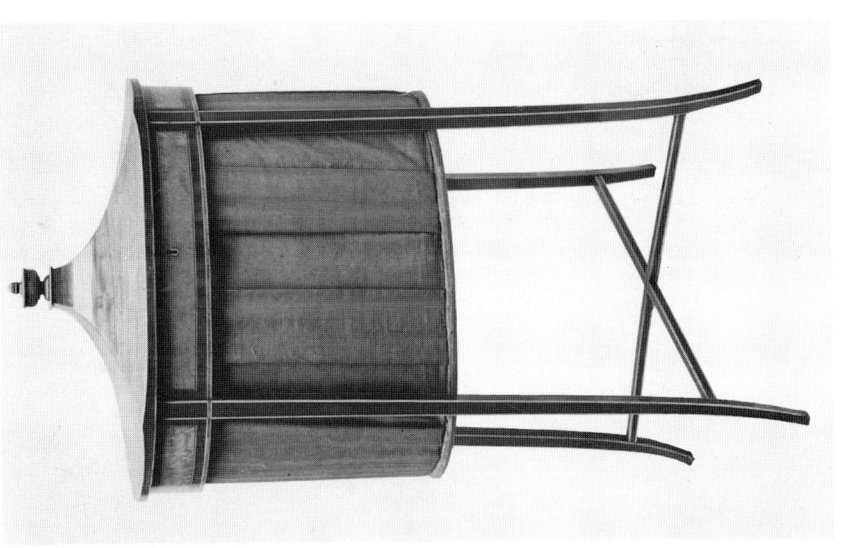

56 REGENCY PAGODA-ROOF WORK TABLE.

PLATE 26

59 INTERIOR VIEW WITH REGENCY ORMOLU-GALLERIED TRIPOD TABLE. *Vide* also H. Clifford Smith, *Buckingham Palace*, 280, a related example "Acquired by Queen Mary"; and *Dictionary of English Furniture*, (rev. ed.) Vol. 3, 201.

PLATE 27

60   REGENCY INLAID SYCAMORE OCTAGONAL CENTER TABLE.

61   REGENCY INLAID SATINWOOD AND EBONY PEMBROKE TABLE. Victoria & Albert Museum. Crown Copyright.

PLATE 28

62 REGENCY MAHOGANY GAMING TABLE WITH TASSEL CAPITALS.

PLATE 29

63 REGENCY INLAID SATINWOOD CARLTON HOUSE TABLE. The handles replacing an original set undoubtedly of the distinctive angular bail pattern illustrated in R. W. Symonds, *Furniture Making in 17th and 18th Century England*, Fig. 183; in Margaret Jourdain, *Regency Furniture*, Fig. 128; and in an advertised example "with original (lever) locks, formerly the property of the Duke of Leeds, Hornby Castle."

PLATE 30

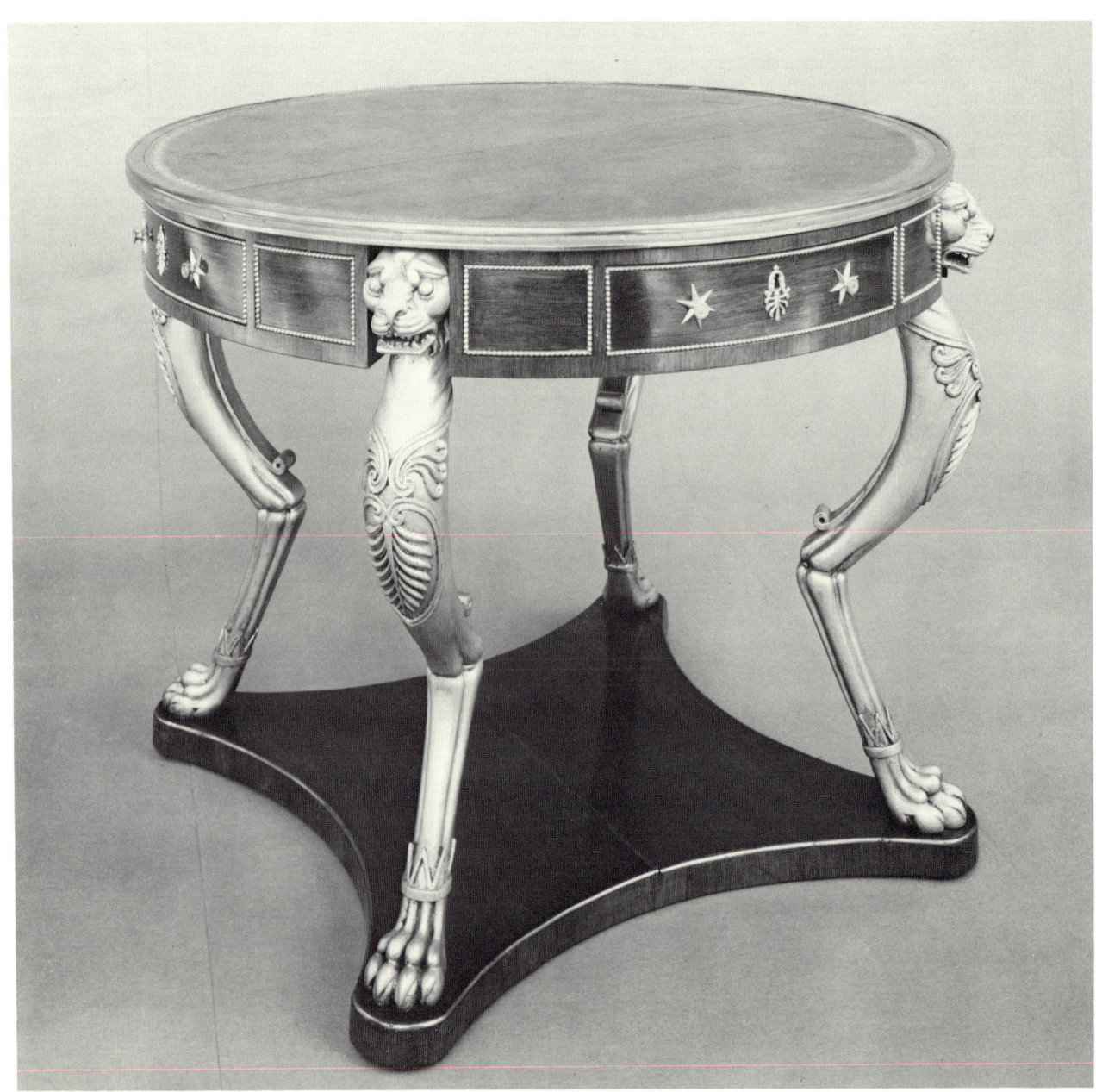

64 REGENCY PARCEL-GILDED MAHOGANY CENTER TABLE WITH ORMOLU MOUNTS. *Vide* also the identical details of R. W. Symonds, *Furniture Making in 17th and 18th Century England*, Fig. 187; *Dictionary of English Furniture*, Vol. 3, Fig. 24; and Margaret Jourdain, *Regency Furniture*, Fig. 101, "From the Marquess of Northampton, Castle Ashby."

PLATE 31

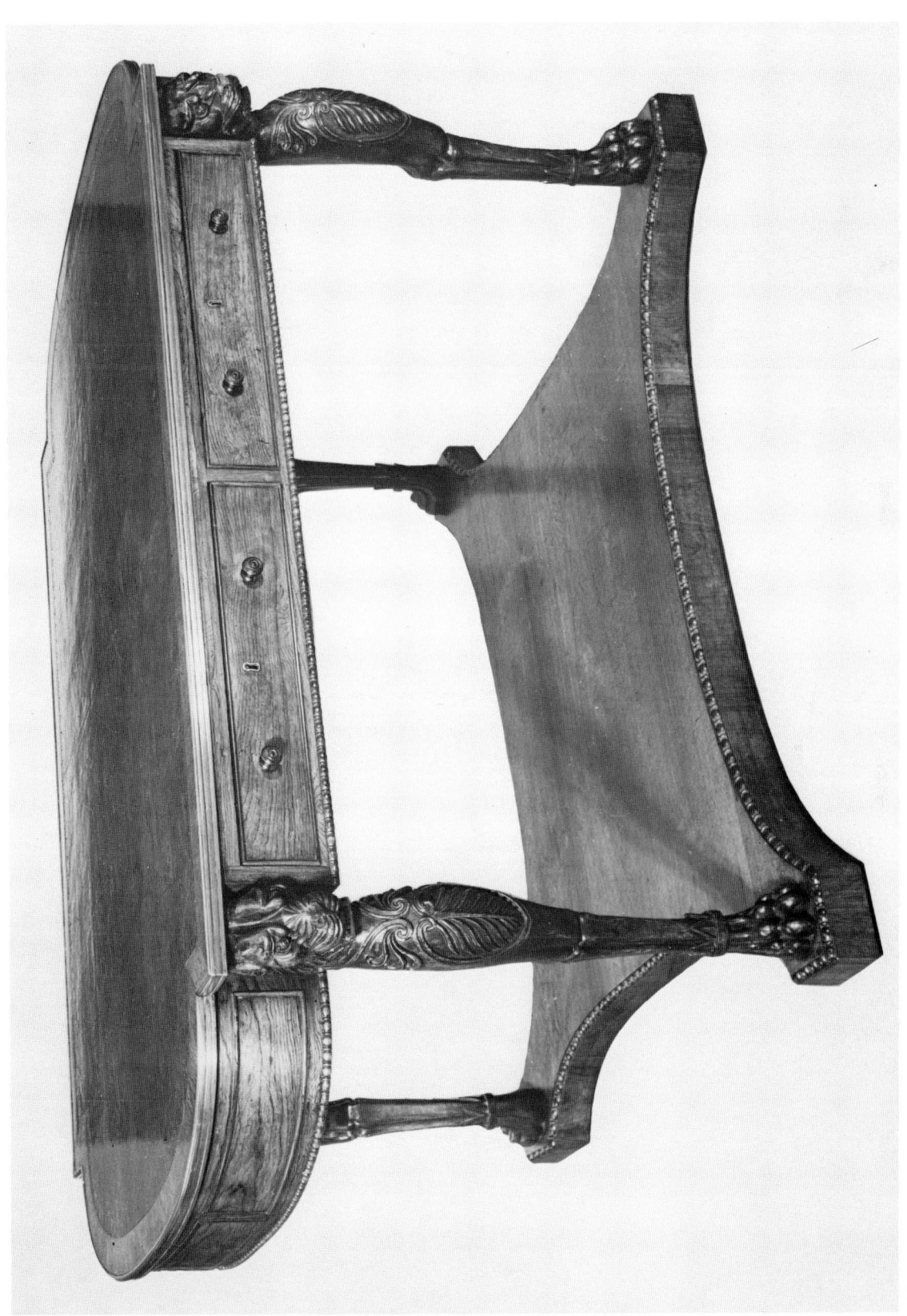

65 REGENCY ROSEWOOD LIBRARY TABLE.

PLATE 32

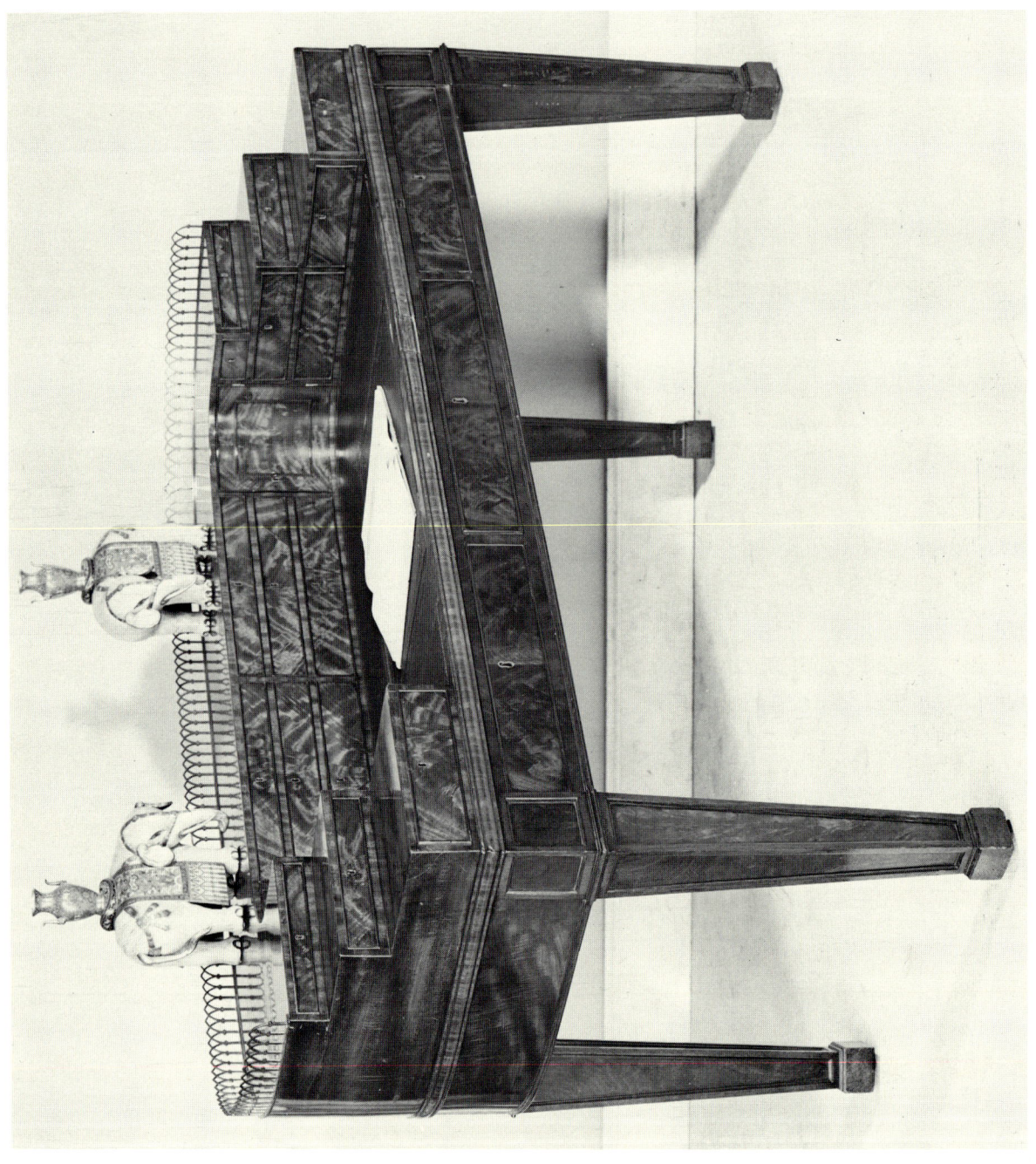

66 REGENCY MAHOGANY CARLTON HOUSE TABLE WITH ORMOLU GALLERY.

PLATE 33

67 REGENCY ROSEWOOD AND IVORY TAMBOUR WRITING TABLE WITH ORMOLU GALLERY.

PLATE 34

68   REGENCY INLAID MAHOGANY CARD TABLE.

69   REGENCY INLAID MAHOGANY OPEN-SHELF SIDE TABLE.

PLATE 35

70 REGENCY INLAID MAHOGANY CARD TABLE.

71 REGENCY INLAID SATINWOOD CARD TABLE. Cf. *Dictionary of English Furniture*, Vol. 3, Fig. 10. Courtesy of J. J. Wolff (Antiques) Ltd., London and New York.

PLATE 36

72 REGENCY CARVED AND GILDED EAGLE CONSOLE. A related example formerly at Duchray Castle, Aberfoyle, Perthshire, Scotland.

73 REGENCY PAINTED AND DECORATED CONSOLE TABLE WITH GILDED GESSO ELEMENTS. The top decorated in the supposed style of Angelica Kauffmann. Victoria & Albert Museum. Crown Copyright.

PLATE 37

75 REGENCY GILDED CONSOLE TABLE WITH GESSO ELEMENTS, THE TOP DECORATED. Cf. *Dictionary of English Furniture*, Vol. 3, Fig. 60, "From Audley End, Essex."

PLATE 38

76 REGENCY INLAID AND DECORATED SATINWOOD SECRETAIRE. With original lever lock, expertized as "Adam, circa 1775." Philadelphia Museum of Art; Loan Exhibition.

PLATE 39

77 REGENCY PAINTED AND DECORTED LOW CABINET
WITH GRILLE PANELS.

78 REGENCY SATINWOOD COMMODE OWNED BY KING GEORGE IV. With painted panels depicting Melpomene, Venus, and Terpsichore. From Carlton House. Exhibited at the Royal Pavilion, Brighton. Collection of Sir William Bennett, K.C.V.O.; F.R.C.S.

PLATE 40

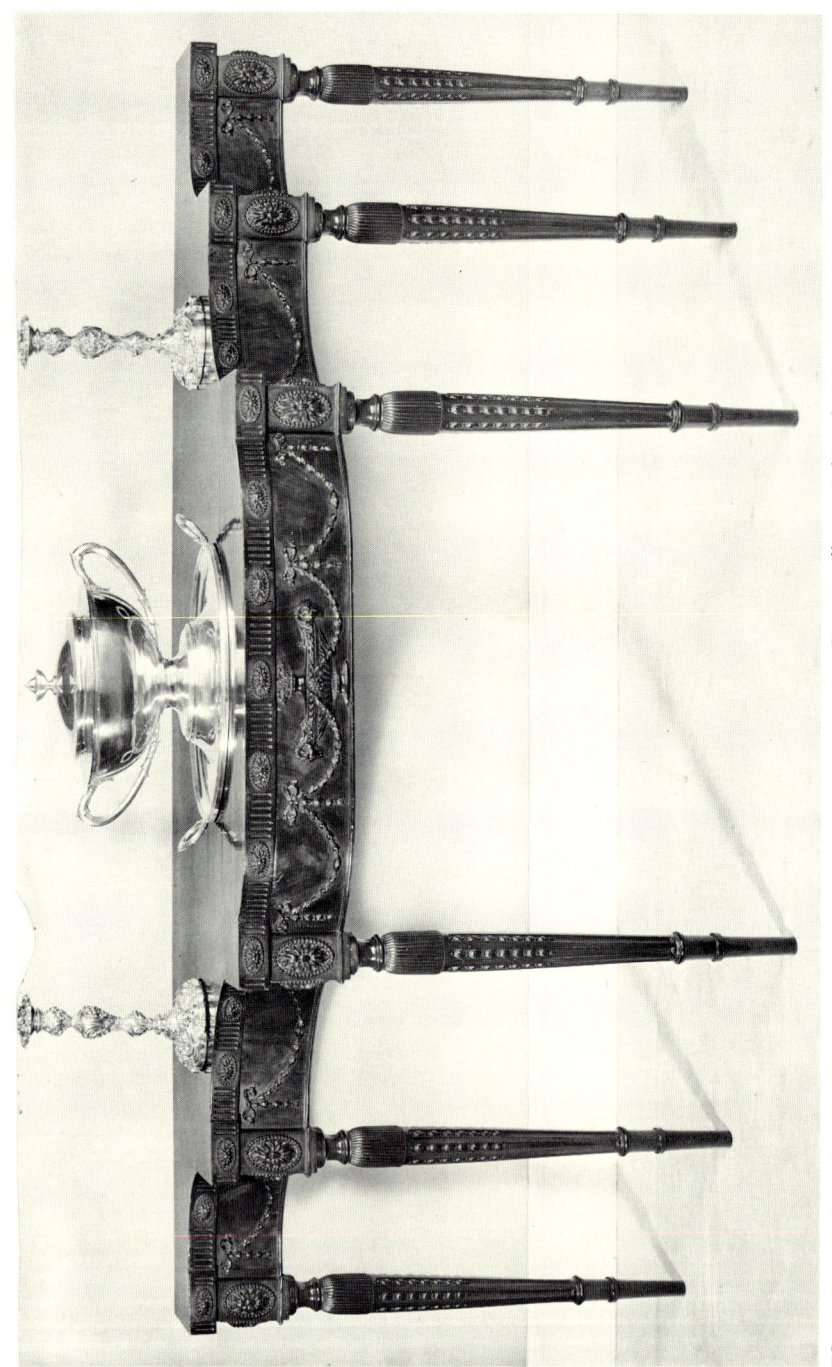

79 REGENCY CARVED MAHOGANY SIDE TABLE WITH TASSEL CAPITALS. Supposedly an Adam design carried out somewhere in England during the eighteenth century.

PLATE 41

80 REGENCY INLAID MAHOGANY SIDEBOARD TABLE WITH PEDESTALS AND URNS.

61

PLATE 42

81 REGENCY INLAID MAHOGANY SIDEBOARD WITH PLATEAU.

PLATE 43

82   REGENCY INLAID MAHOGANY SIDEBOARD WITH PLATEAU.

PLATE 44

83 REGENCY INLAID MAHOGANY SIDEBOARD WITH EGYPTIAN TERMS. Courtesy of Needham's Antiques, Inc., New York City.

PLATE 45

84   REGENCY INLAID MAHOGANY BOW-FRONT CHEST OF DRAWERS WITH ORIGINAL HANDLES AND ESCUTCHEONS.

PLATE 46

85 REGENCY INLAID MAHOGANY BOW-FRONT CHEST OF DRAWERS. Described as an American Hepplewhite example of the late eighteenth century.

86 REGENCY INLAID SATINWOOD COMMODE.

PLATE 47

87 REGENCY INLAID MAHOGANY LOW CABINET WITH ORMOLU TOP EDGING AND GRILLWORK.

88 REGENCY INLAID SATINWOOD LOW CABINET WITH ORMOLU GRILLWORK. Courtesy of Needham's Antiques, Inc., New York City.

PLATE 48

89 REGENCY MARQUETRY COMMODE MOUNTED IN ORMOLU.

90 REGENCY INLAID SATINWOOD LOW CABINET WITH WIRE MESH PANELS.

PLATE 49

91 REGENCY INLAID MAHOGANY OPEN-SHELF CABINET WITH ORMOLU GALLERY AND WIRE-MESH PANELS. *Vide* also *Age of Satinwood*, Fig. 201.

PLATE 50

92 REGENCY INLAID MAHOGANY SECRETAIRE.

PLATE 51

93 REGENCY INLAID ZEBRAWOOD SECRETAIRE WITH EGYPTIAN TERMS. Victoria & Albert Museum. Crown Copyright.

PLATE 52

94 REGENCY INLAID SATINWOOD AND MAHOGANY CLOCK-CABINET. With distinctive astragals, crossetted panels, leaf-carved colonettes, and stepped cresting.

PLATE 53

95 REGENCY BRASS-INLAID EBONY CABINET MOUNTED IN ORMOLU.

PLATE 54

96 REGENCY MAHOGANY BREAKFRONT SECRETARY-BOOKCASE. Cf. pilasters with Ills. 50, 52, 53. Courtesy of Needham's Antiques, Inc., New York City.

PLATE 55

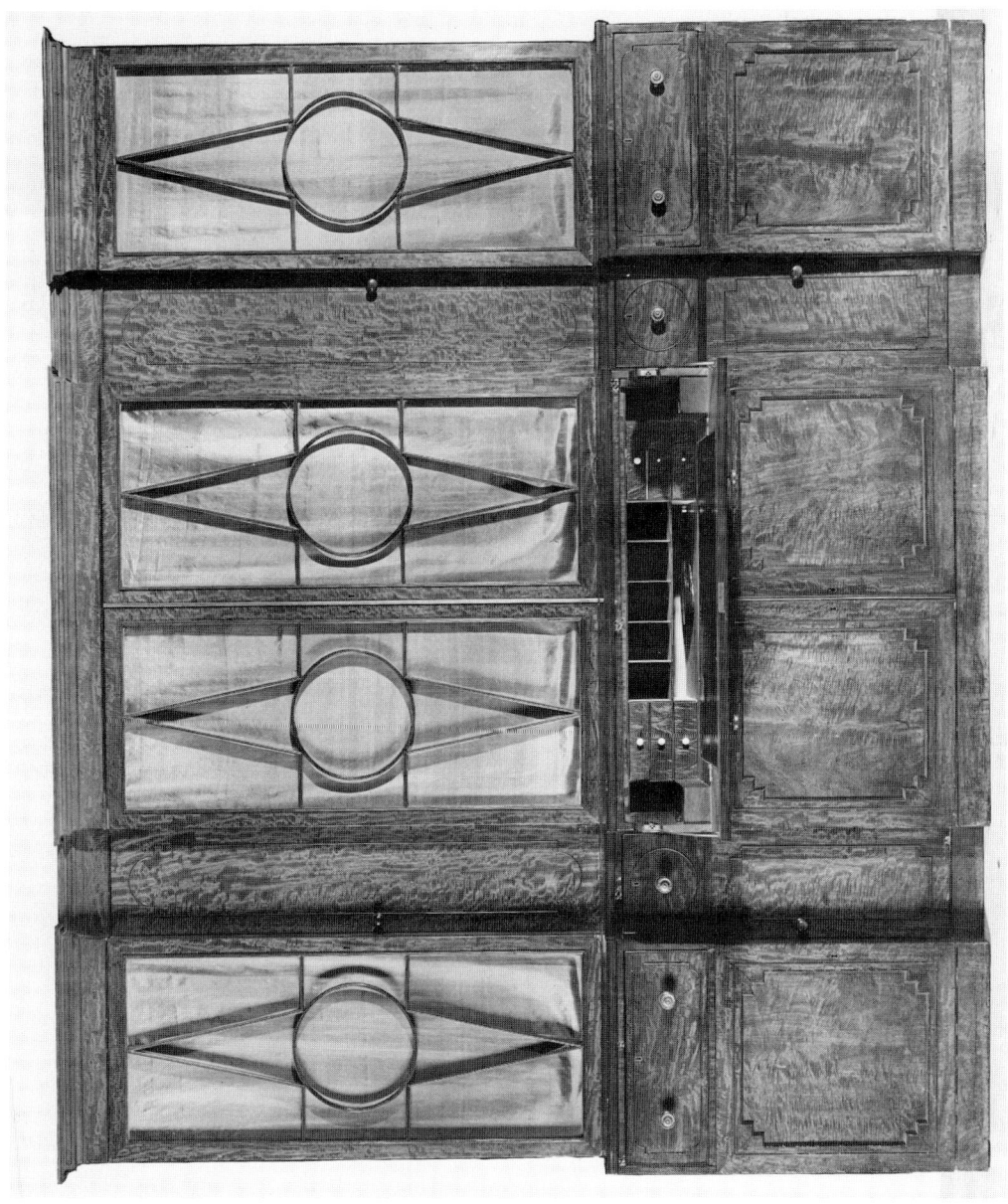

97 REGENCY MAHOGANY BREAKFRONT SECRETARY-BOOKCASE. Sold as "American, circa 1810." From the famous Haskell Collection of Americana.

PLATE 56

98   LATE REGENCY YEWWOOD TAVERN CHAIR.

99   CHIPPENDALE CARVED MAHOGANY SIDE CHAIR.

PLATE 57

100 DECORATED LACQUER BONHEUR DU JOUR. M. Beurdeley, Paris, Circa 1870.

PLATE 58

101 LATE CHIPPENDALE PARCEL-GILDED MAHOGANY WALL MIRROR. Courtesy of Needham's Antiques, Inc., New York City.

PLATE 59

102-103   GEORGE III YEWWOOD ARMCHAIR AND SIDE CHAIR.

104-105   PAIR OF SO-CALLED WESTMORLAND OR YORKSHIRE ARMCHAIRS.

Index

[Italic figures refer to illustrations]

Aberfoyle, 14, *72*
Admiralty House, *39*
Age of Mahogany, 11, 13, 14
Age of Satinwood, 3, *91*
Age of Walnut, 12
America, 10
American (misnomer), 15, *85*, *97*
Americana, importing dealer in, 15
American cabinetwork, 15
American furniture, 10, 15
American furniture makers, 15
American timber, 10
Andaman Islands, 17
Antiques World, 5
Arm terminals, 13, 17
Arm terminals, whorled, 6, 11
Artes des Bois, Les, 16
Athol, Duke of, 10
Audley End, *75*

Badminton House, 13
Beaufort, Duke of, 13
Bennett, Sir William, *78*
Beurdeley, M., 16, *100*
Bird's-eye maple, 10
Blaise Castle, 14
Boulle, Charles André, 6
Boxwood, 11
Bristol, ii, 14
British furniture, 7, 8
British royal family, 1
Bronze doré, 12
Buckingham Palace, 15, *59*
Burma, 17

Cabinet Maker's Assistant, The, 8, 9, 10, 11
Calamander, *30*
Caledon, Earl of, *45*
Canton, 17
Carlton House, *78*
Castle Ashby, *64*
Castlecoole, *54*
Ceylon, 17
Channon, John, 1, 5, 6, 7, 8, 11, 14
Channon Pieces (misnomer), 5, 6, 7, 8, 11, 14
Charlotte, Princess, 3
Charlotte, Queen, 3, 10

China, 17
Chinese characters, 17
Chinese craftsmen, 17
Chinoiserie, *44*
Chippendale, Thomas, 3, 4, 13, 14
Churchill, Lady Randolph, 17
Copped Hall, 13
Country Life, 6, *54*
Cressent, Charles, 12

DeLisle and Dudley, Lord, 13
Designs speak for themselves, 8, 13
Dickson, R. Eden, 14
Dictionary of English Furniture, 4, 7, 15, *31*, *51*, *59*, *64*, *71*, *75*
Director, Chippendale's, 8, 13
Directory of Queen Anne, Early Georgian & Chippendale Furniture, 6
Directory of the Historic Cabinet Woods, 7, 9, 10
Dolphin supports, *44*
Dorset, 14
Dublin, 1, 3, 4, 5, 8, 9, 10, 11, 12
Dublin antique shops, 13
Dublin patterns, 17
Dublin shops, 4
Dublin Windsor chairs, 15
Duchray Castle, 14, *72*

"Eagle Pier Tables," 14
Early Federal cabinetwork, 15
East Indian rosewood, 17
Edwards and Jourdain, 4, 13
Egyptian terms, 12, *39*, *83*, *93*
English (misnomer), 1, 11, 12, 16
English Furniture: The Georgian Period, 12, 15, *37*, *54*
European fashion, 17
Evidence, contrived, 1, 8

Fane, Sir Spencer Ponsonby, 12, 13, *13-15*
France, Made in, 5, 6
Furniture-Making in 17th and 18th Century England, 12, *63*, *64*

Georgian Cabinet-Makers, 4, 5, 7, 10, 13
Gillingham, John, 9
Gillow factory, 17
Gloucestershire, 13, 14
Grendy, Giles, 13

Handles, angular bail, *63*
Handles, original, *84*
Harris, M., catalogue, 5
Haskell Collection, *97*
Hayward, John, 5, 7
Hepplewhite, Sheraton & Regency Furniture, 15
Holly, 11, *38*
Hope, Thomas, *37*
Hornby Castle, *63*
Horse flesh, 9
Horseflesh mahogany, 9

India, 17
Ireland, 17
Irish, 8, 12
Irish petit point, 13

Jennie, 17
Jourdain, Margaret, 12, *25, 29, 33, 39, 45, 63, 64*
Jourdain and Rose, 12, 15, *37, 54*

Kauffmann, Angelica, *73*
Kearney, Joshua, 3
King George IV, *78*

Laburnum, 9, 10
Lancaster, 17
Langlois, Pierre, 1, 5
Langlois pieces, 11
Lannuier, Charles Honoré, 12, *45*
Late Chippendale, 4, 15, 16, *101*
Leeds, Duke of, *63*
Lever locks, 15, *54, 63, 76*
Limerick, Dowager Countess of, 15
Liverpool, 8
London (misnomer), 1, 5
London commode, so-called, 5
London craftsmen, 4
London productions, 4-5

Mack, John, 4
Mack, Williams, and Gibton, 3-4
Macquoid, Percy, 3, 11, 12, 13, 14, 15, 17
Maker to His Majesty, 3
Makers to His Majesty, 4
Martin, Ralph G., 17
Mary, Queen, 15, 59
Masters, William, 10
Metropolitan Furniture of the Georgian Years, 5, 6
Mirror-back pier table, *45*
Montgomeryshire, *35*
Morgan, J. Pierpont, *3*

National Art Collections Fund, 5
Nelson, Lord, *51*
Nelsonian, *4, 39*
Newton Park, 14
New York, 10, *43, 45*
Northampton, Marquis of, *64*
North German or Danish, 17
Nostel Priory, 13

Old English Furniture (misnomer), 1, 3, 12, 17
Oriental armchairs, 17

Padauk, 10, 17, *26*
Paris, *100*
Pennsylvania, 10
Penshurst Place, 13
Perthshire, 14, *72*
Philadelphia, *9*
Philadelphia craftsmen, 9
Plumwood, 10
Powderham Castle, 5, 7
Powis, Earl of, *35*

Record price, 5
Regency Furniture, 11-12, *25, 33, 39, 45, 63, 64*
Roentgen, Abraham, 5
Rosewood, 10-11
Russian Market, 5

Sabicu, 8-9, *35*
St. Giles House, 14
St. Oswald, Lord, 13
Salem, *41*
Shaftesbury, Earl of, 14
Smith, H. Clifford, *59*
Sonnenberg Collection, 16
Sotheby Parke-Bernet, 16
Symonds, R. W., 10, 11, 12, 14, 17, *63, 64*

Tassel capitals, *62, 79*
Tavern chair, 9, *98*
Teahan, John, 3, 4, 5

Victoria & Albert Museum Bulletin, 5
Vile, William, 4, 5, 10

W. F., maker's initials, 13
Walnut, Virginia, 9
Weekes' Cabinets, 7
Weekes' Museum Titchborne Street, 7
Weekes' Museum Cabinets, 8, 11, 14, *94*
Wellington, Duke of, 12, *39*
Westmorland, 17
Windsor armchairs, 9
Wood pegs, 17

Yew, 9
Yewwood, Irish, 9, 17, *98*
Yorkshire chairs, 17

Zebrawood, *93*